Guide to Investing in the NIGERIAN STOCK MARKET

ALEX UWAJEH

Legal Disclaimers and Copyright

This book is presented to you for informational purposes only and is not a substitution for any professional advice. The contents herein are based on the views and opinions of the author and all associated contributors.

While every effort has been made by the author and all associated contributors to present accurate and up to date information within this document, it is apparent technologies rapidly change.

Therefore, the author and all associated contributors reserve the right to update the contents and information provided herein as these changes progress. The author and/or all associated contributors take no responsibility for any errors or omissions if such discrepancies exist within this document.

The author and all other contributors accept no responsibility for any consequential actions taken, whether monetary, legal, or otherwise, by any and all readers of the materials provided. It is the readers sole responsibility to seek professional advice before taking any action on their part.

Readers results will vary based on their skill level and individual perception of the contents herein, and thus no guarantees, monetarily or otherwise, can be made accurately. Therefore, no guarantees are made.

As always, I give God all the glory for the completion of this book.

Table of Contents

An Introduction to the Nigerian Stock Market

The Nigerian Stock exchange was established in 1960 and trading began in 1961 with just 19 securities available for trade. However, the market has seen amazing growth and has become one of the fastest growing stock exchanges in Africa, providing investors with plenty of excellent opportunities.

The Exchange is regulated by the SEC (Securities and Exchange Commission), which was established in 1999 through the Investment and Securities Act. It acts as the regulating body, setting prices for securities of newly established private companies, takes part in developing the Nigerian capital market, and regulates the operators on the Nigerian capital market and much more.

Trading or investing on the Nigerian Stock Exchange is quite similar to trading on the

stock exchanges of most countries, at least in terms of technicalities.
An investor has to be willing to research and analyze the companies whose stocks they are considering investing or trading just like they would in any other country.

The advantage of investing in Nigerian companies, though, is that it is still considered an emerging market and is currently experiencing amazing growth.

This means that investors can purchase stocks at reasonable prices and obtain a much better ROI than if they were to invest in an established market like the U.S. or Europe.

Generally, investors will be able to stretch their cash further, as well, allowing them to spread their portfolio out so they are not wholly investing in a single company or industry.

What is stock market?

A stock market is where company stock is traded between people who want to buy the stock and people who want to sell stock. The Nigerian Stock Exchange has turned out to be the toast of investors the world over. This has resulted in foreign investors investing huge sums of money in the Nigerian Stock Exchange. Shares and stock are different words but in the stock market world, they often mean the same thing. For example you could say "I have shares in Flour mills " or "I have stock in Flour mills ". Therefore if you see stock and share used it is important not to get confused as they both often mean the same thing.

However if you were to clearly define the two; stock is the capital raised by a company through the issue of shares. A share is a single unit of stock.

What is dividend?

A dividend is the payment an investor receives from the company he/she is currently investing in.
The company pays the dividend from the profit it generates throughout its financial year. As a result, if the company fails to make a profit, dividends are not likely to be received by the investor. The dividend is normally paid in two parts, an interim and a final dividend.

Bonus Share

A bonus share is a freeshare of stock given to current/existing shareholders in a company, based upon the number of shares that the shareholder already owns at the time of announcement of the bonus.

IPO

Initial Public Offering. The first sale of stock by a company to the public.

Companies offering an IPO are sometimes new, young companies, or sometimes companies which have been around for many years but are finally deciding to go public. IPOs are often risky investments, but often have the potential for significant gains. IPOs are often used as a way for a young company to gain necessary market capital.

What is eDividend?

eDividend is a service which allows your registrar to electronically pay your cash dividend entitlements directly into your bank account instead of making payment via bank cheques. One of the main objectives of implementing eDividend is to promote greater efficiency of the payment system. Common problems such as delay receipt of dividend cheques, lost cheques, cheques expired, etc. will be eliminated.

How do I register for eDividend?

To register, complete the relevant prescribed form which can be obtained from either your stock broker's office or download from registrar's website, fill the form and authorise, signed and stamp by your bank, finally submit the form to your registrar.

What is CSCS (Central Securities Clearing System)

This is a clearing house of the Nigerian stock exchange. It contains information about stock movements, prices and other data relating to stock transactions in the Nigerian stock market.

Factors that Affect the Stock Market

There are many factors that affect the stock market, however below is a list of the main factors.

- ✓ Interest rates
- ✓ Employment rates
- ✓ The property market
- ✓ Oil prices
- ✓ War
- ✓ Natural disasters
- ✓ Big company mergers
- ✓ Big company buy outs
- ✓ Good/bad company news

Opportunity for the Smart Investor

Investing in high dividend stocks can be a great investment. There are many reasons for that. One of the main reason is compounding interest.

You will get a higher yield if you have high dividend stocks as part of your investment portfolio. This yield is then reinvested.
This process of reinvesting repeats itself for as long as you own the stocks.
As the interest on your investment is compounded, it will greatly increase your return on these investments.

The other reason why many investors have high dividend stocks in their portfolio is their stability.

But before investing in a high dividend stock, it is advisable to go through the dividend history as well as the stock price history.

Buy shares that regularly pay you to invest - that is, those that pay good dividends.

Dividends are always king. And in my view, companies that add shareholders to their payrolls are good shares to own. Yes, a dividend stock can get hit in a bear market just like any other.

However, according to Standard & Poor, dividend payers outperformed non payers. When you ride through the years of bull and bear markets, dividend stocks have a historically proven edge.

Choosing High Income Portfolio

Stick to the big fish: The reason is simple: security. It's not rocket science... we're in this long-term, and large caps have more chance of outliving small caps.

Solid History: The idea is to locate shares that have a proven history of delivering income growth even in years when profits may fall temporarily.

Steer Clear of Debt: Financial problems start with too much debt, so you can avoid that problem by preferring low-debt companies if possible.

Sector Diversification: Critical. If your portfolio is to weather even the toughest storms over the years, your risk must be evenly spread. Put simply, this is the most sensible strategy for wealth accumulation.

Trading Strategies

A popular trading strategy is to sell sufficient shares to realize your initial investment. So say you bought 10,000 units in UBA Plc at 5 Naira. You could now sell about 3,600 unit at 14 Naira to take back the money that you originally invested.
That would leave you with 6,400 units that have effectively cost you nothing. This does make you feel good and allows you to sleep soundly at night.

In the end this is a matter of balancing your portfolio and deciding how much risk you are prepared to take in any one share.

Don't Be Afraid to Bank Profits

If I buy a share at 50 kobo it is because I think it will go to, say 2 Naira?

It makes sense to sell at least some of the shares and bank some profit. You can never be entirely sure what lies around the next corner.

When I buy a share for the first time, I usually start by making just a small investment perhaps no more than a quarter of what I might eventually hold and as confidence builds I can add to my initial holding until I have enough.

Investing in the Nigerian Stock Market by Nigerian Investors in Diaspora

The last couple of years have seen a huge sum of money being pumped into the

Nigerian Stock Market. This is partly as a result of keen interest by Nigerians in diaspora.

How can Nigerians in Diaspora Invest in the Nigerian Stock Market?

Issues to be looked at include which stockbroker and stocks? Getting dividend payments, most importantly, how to keep an eye on your portfolio irrespective of where you are located.

It is imperative for investors to engage with broking firms that provide online services,

so that they can view orders, view price improvements as well as issue trade instructions on their portfolios.
Stock management account is usually opened with a fee from N50,000.

However, individual firms set fees for various services, which are subject to conditions.

The fee is then used to purchase requested shares. It is advisable for investors to research a company before investing in Nigerian stocks.

Please note that all stocks profiled here will fluctuate at one point or another. A stock that performed badly or well in the past could perform well or badly in the future. Investors are advised not to assume that all views, opinions or recommendations will produce profitable results. Hence research is of an importance.

How to Make Money from the Stock Market

There are, essentially, two ways you can make money from the stock exchange: capital appreciation and dividends. Capital appreciation refers to the rise in price of your shares, allowing you to make a profit if or when you sell them.

The route you take depends on your personal style but, generally speaking, dividend stocks will allow you to enjoy the best of both worlds, namely capital appreciation and dividends.
You will be able to enjoy some of your profits right away through dividends and if you reinvest those dividends in more stocks, you can further build your investment portfolio without having to use your personal cash to do it.

However, keep in mind that dividends can and do change.

A company paying out dividends today might not do so in five years time. However, any form of investing has some form of risk attached to it but dividend stocks generally are considered to be a lower risk investment due to the stability of the companies.

When you invest in Nigerian stock market, you are investing in a market that has high growth potential. Nigerian stocks can be a better and more affordable choice for anyone, including those with limited capital.

With as little as 45,000 Naira to invest, you can acquire more shares of your favourite Nigerian stocks, compared to only a few shares in European and American shares.

Nigerian stocks give investors the opportunity to earn a high return on their investment over a short period of time.
It is common for investors to earn a return of 2000% on Nigerian stocks.

However, holding on to some of these stocks for the long term can often bring you even greater profits.

Indeed, with my personal investments, my largest wins with Nigerian stocks actually came only after I had held the shares for a couple of years. When those gains happened, however, the price explosions were tremendous and it was over the course of a few months.

When you are making gains like that in Nigerian stock market, it seems that patience is a virtue. No matter if it takes one year or five, if a stock goes big time, turning hundreds of Naira into many thousands, or thousands into hundreds of thousands, then the results were definitely worth the wait.

The companies are just as strong, execute their business plans just as well, and have the same upside potential they always have. Only now, they are trading at bargain prices.

Don't let market risk scare you out of your investments.
Get involved with solid, fundamentally sound Nigerian stocks and be patient with them.

Market risk is also a good buying opportunity, since quality stocks are trading on the cheap and you are currently looking at one of the best times in recent history to get involved in Nigerian stocks.

Why Invest in the Nigerian Stock Market?

The Nigerian stock market presents some highly attractive opportunities for investors due to a number of reasons. Historically, Nigeria was never considered a good investment opportunity, especially since the country was closed to foreign investors and was under military dictatorship. Subsequently, though, once it returned to democratic rule, legislature was enforced that abolished all regulations limiting access to foreign investments.

Thus, with the new governmental system in place, Nigeria was able to flourish economically and establish trade and relations with foreign investors from all over the world.

The change in legislation led to a capital market boom that was almost record-breaking once investors from all over the world gained access to Nigeria.

Nigeria's economy has experienced significant growth, at an average rate of 7% from 2005-2009, experiencing a spike in 2010 as the real growth rate climbed to 8.4%. In 2011, growth contracted slightly to an estimated 6.9% according to Global Finance but it is still an impressive number considering the global economic situation. This growth is mainly due to an influx of foreign investments.

Thanks to the oil industry, many other sectors have developed and are experiencing significant growth, including the financial sector, which makes for a very interesting investment in Nigeria. A quick look at the Nigerian stock market shows most banks holding strong, despite the crash experienced by the stock market in 2009.

Despite the latter, Nigerian companies continued to pay out dividends and while the market hasn't fully recovered, the Nigerian All-Share Index has remained relatively stable ever since.

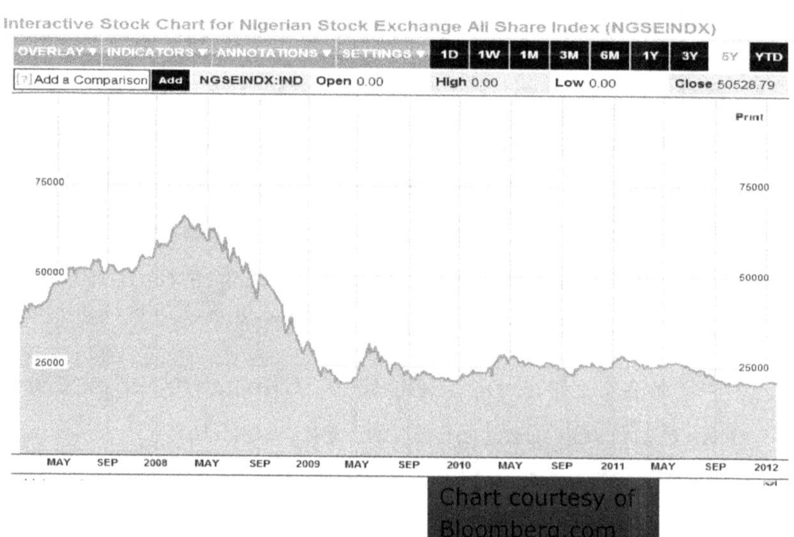

Chart courtesy of Bloomberg.com

Africa, in general, has become an excellent opportunity for foreign investors due to the financial meltdown and continuing recession. Any investor looking to diversify their investment portfolio should certainly consider Nigeria since it's likely its GDP will continue to grow for the foreseeable future as various industries and other sectors develop and an increasing number of companies move into the country due to relatively low labour costs.

One advantage to investing in Nigeria is that investors won't be putting their capital into exotic financial products but into tangible and real sectors of the economy, including residential construction and more.

Another benefit is the low entry level compared to more established markets as shares are still relatively cheap but offer great potential for both capital appreciation and cash flow as dividend yields are quite attractive.

While there is often social unrest in Nigeria, this shouldn't act as a deterrent. In fact, it could present unique opportunities for the savvy investor because while stock prices will drop during these periods, they do recover and dividend yields remain relatively unchanged.

In other words, investors can get into the market at bargain prices and enjoy their profits as soon as the market rebounds.

The chart below shows how the market reacted to the January 2012 strike in relation to doubling fuel prices. The market began to fall around the beginning of the month only to rally towards the middle of January when issues had seemed to be resolved. However, the nation-wide strike started up again around the 18th and the market reflected this in another dive.

At the end of the month, the market began to rally as the Nigerian government dropped fuel prices and labour unions officially ended the strikes. Clearly, the dips in the market would have been excellent opportunities for any investor to enter the market.

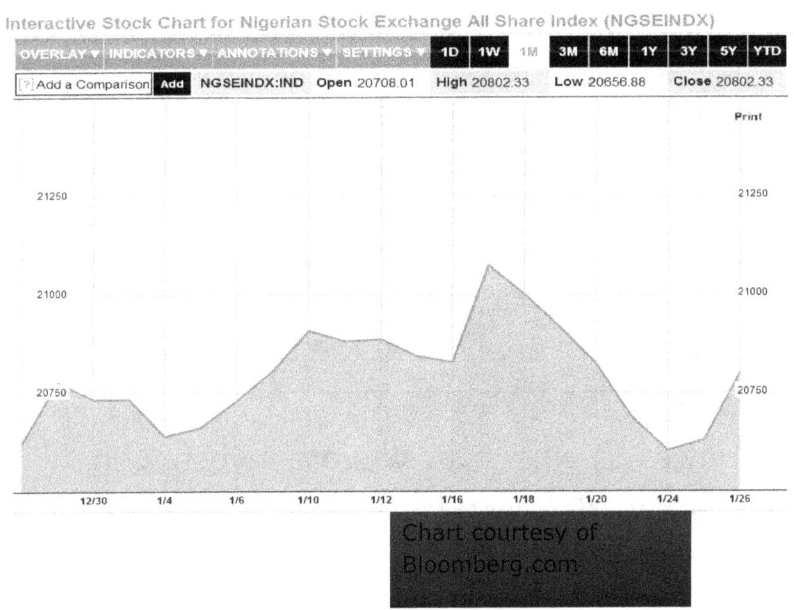

Chart courtesy of Bloomberg.com

Do I Have to Do Something Special to Invest in the Nigerian Stock Market?

When it comes to investing in the Nigerian stock market, you basically need to follow the same rules that apply to any other stock market, whether it's established or an emerging one. This means taking the time to get to know the economy of the country, gaining a deep understanding of the sector or industry you are considering and conducting an in-depth analysis of the company you are considering investing in.

However, whenever you are investing in Nigeria, you need to choose a reputable broker to work with. Luckily, the Nigerian stock market is well organized and the SEC provides a list of authorized operators on their website, allowing you to easily choose a good stock broker to work with.

Investing in Stocks

Now that we've established that the Nigerian stock market holds endless potential and can offer a great return on your investment, you are probably itching to get started. However, you're first going to have to lay some groundwork, which includes setting goals for your investment strategy.

For example, if your goal is to have a comfortable retirement, then you need to work out approximately how much money you need to live on and when you want to retire. By establishing your objectives now, it will be easier for you to come up with a practical investment plan to achieve your goals.

Making a Plan

The first step to designing an investment plan is to understand yourself.

If you want to succeed as an investor, you have to learn how to save money. You will need some capital to start out with, and once you do, you need to decide what type of investor you are.

Note, though, that you should never invest money you need for short-term goals in long-term investments. For example, don't invest the money for next month's rent in stocks because even if they are liquid and you can sell them quickly, the timing might not be right and you could even incur a loss. So, it's always best to keep back enough money to see you through some months of living expenses, just in case the worst happens and you lose your regular source of income. Remember, that as an investor you are in it for the long haul, your goal being to preserve your capital as well as to increase it.

This is slightly riskier than putting your cash in a savings account but you are definitely more careful than the trader, whose only goal is to see short-term profits. Thus, your strategy will be formulated over several years and you have to learn to look at the bigger picture.

In general, you will probably be holding on to your investments for at least five years, which means that you will have to do extensive research because you want to invest in a company that is stable and has proven sustainable success.

The advantage of long-term investing is that your investments have a time to grow and are less likely to be affected by the inherent short-term volatility of the financial markets. So, now you have to decide what type of investor you are. You can be either conservative or aggressive, which usually refers to the mix of investments in your portfolio.

For example, someone who is more conservative will tend to play it safe and allocate half of their portfolio, or even less, to equities, while the remainder will consist of lower risk investments such as savings accounts and treasury bonds.

It is usually recommended that the closer you get to retirement, the more conservative your investment strategy should be because you have less time to recover from a market crash. The younger you are though, the more leeway you have and you can take a slightly more aggressive approach, which will allow you to see faster gains.

Aggressive investors tend to go for 70% of their portfolio in equities and 30% in lower risk investments. This is a growth strategy, allowing for faster gains and can be quite lucrative, especially if the returns are reinvested.

Understanding The Market And Becoming A Value Investor

When you find a stock that could potentially be a hidden gem, you have to ask yourself some questions. You need to look at the price and determine whether or not it is so low because of an economic slowdown.
This is easy to tell as most other stocks will be down as well but if the company fundamentals remain strong, in other words they're still profitable and their sales haven't dropped dramatically, this may be just the stock you're looking for.

Another reason the price of a particular stock could be down is because of bad results in the industry. When bad news comes out, traders tend to offload stocks in that particular field but if the company you are looking at still has good results, then their stock is an excellent option for the value investor.

However, if the price of stock is down because the company itself is experiencing problems, such as declining sales or earnings, high levels of debt, poor cash flow, illegalities and so on, then you shouldn't even consider making a purchase.

Picking Potential Winners

Knowledge is power and nowhere does this hold more truth than in investing. The more you know about an industry, the company and its stock, the more likely you are to make a wise investment decision. The more information you have, the better the chance of maximizing your return on investment and reducing your exposure to risk.

This is especially important in an emerging market like Nigeria where there are many more factors at play that can influence the markets, especially political and social issues.

Understand the Market You Are Investing In

Investing in any financial market involves reading financial statements. However, most investors limit themselves to corporate financial statements and overlook sovereign statements.

In other words, they only take the micro view, looking at the company's financials without taking the time to look at the bigger picture.

Some of the most important metrics include a country's GDP or Gross Domestic Product. This figure reveals everything a country produces, including goods and services.

Likewise, you should consider analyzing the budget, to determine which sectors will be allocated funds for development. This is especially important in an emerging economy like Nigeria where there is still a lot of work to be done in terms of construction. A high investment budget in infrastructure will mean growth in the construction industry and all inter-connected services.

Get to Know the Industry

A good investor will focus on industry they know and understand, carry out due diligence and indept research before they decide to start evaluating individual companies.

It is hard to evaluate the performance of a company if you don't understand how the industry functions and being knowledgeable about the industry in question and how well the company you are evaluating is positioned in it, can make or break you in the long run.

A good example is the recent financial crisis. Before the meltdown, investors were convinced that the financial sector was untouchable. By getting to know the sector as well as the company very well,

you are in a position to make better investment decisions. For example, if you work in the fast-moving consumer goods sector, you are more aware of which companies perform better, how effective their sales teams are and so on. Additionally, by working in the industry you can often learn of important information that can impact dividends and share price, such as new regulations. While this information is usually public knowledge, most investors that aren't familiar with the industry will overlook it. Of course, you can consider any sector you are interested in as long as you are willing to put in the time and effort to do the research. This is why it is often a good idea to choose sectors you are passionate about.
For example, if you love reading, you might consider the publishing sector.

The key is to soak up as much information as you can about the industry you are targeting.

The more you know about the industry, the easier it will be to identify potentially good dividend stocks and the better your investment decisions will be.

Additionally, never take anything at face value and check all the information you find against other sources that are credible.

Just because one expert recommends a certain company's stock, that doesn't mean it is necessarily so. Always double and triple check everything before you jump in.

However, it is also important to diversify your portfolio. This means that even if you are an expert on a particular industry, you should look to other companies and sectors as well because you don't want to put all your eggs in one basket.

Now that you know the importance of understanding the industry as a whole, let's take a look on how to evaluate individual dividend stocks so you can make wise investment decisions.

Fundamentals

Clearly, you need to learn how to look at a company's financial information and determine whether or not it is a good candidate to invest in.

Luckily, all this information is readily available since all companies that are publicly traded have to publish all their most important facts and figures, which are usually contained in a range of reports, including an annual report and a quarterly report. This information is usually readily available, either via the Nigerian stock exchange website or on the company's official site.

Technical Analysis

The fundamentals will provide you with the data you need to identify if there is an opportunity. However, technical data is just

as critical because this data will let you know when to enter the market.
No matter what your objective is, whether capital appreciation or cash flow, you want to enter the market at a point where you will make a profit either way and the only way to do that is through technical analysis.

No matter what combination of indicators you use, you need to be objective. In fact, it's often best to take a proven method and apply it. Technical analysis is a massive topic and there are more indicators than you can shake a stick at.

It will take time to understand and master but it is necessary. If you want to build up a nice nest egg for your retirement and to avoid losing all your capital, learning how to analyze price charts is a vital skill.

Companies that Offer Solid Dividends

I have identified some companies with solid dividend yields based on consistent dividend payout, financial strength and bonus shares.

Note: Your capital is at risk when you invest in shares - you can lose some or all of your money, so never risk more than you can afford to lose. Always seek professional advice if you are unsure about the suitability of any investment. Past performance is not a reliable indicator of future results.

Banking Sector

First Bank Nigeria Plc

Guaranty Trust Bank

Zenith International Bank Plc

Breweries Sector

Guinness

Nigerian Breweries PLC

Building Materials Sector

Ashaka Cement

Cement Company of Northern Nigeria (CCNN)

Dangote Cement

West African Portland Cement Plc (WapCo)

Chemical and Paints Sector

CAP PLC

Conglomerates Sector

PZ Industries Plc

U A C Nigeria PLC

Unilever Nigeria PLC

Construction Sector

Julius Berger PLC

Foods, Beverages, and Tobacco Sector

7up Nigeria PLC

Dangote Flour Mills PLC

Dangote Sugar Refinery PLC

Flour Mills Nigeria PLC

Nestle Nigeria PLC

Healthcare Sector

Glaxo smithkline consumer Nigeria Plc

Petroleum Sector

ConOil Plc

Oando Plc

Mobil Oil Nigeria Plc

Total Nigeria Plc

Printing and Publishing Sector

UPL

Longman

Real Estate Sector

UAC-property

Promising Growth Stocks:

✓OkomuOil

✓Access Bank of Nigeria Plc

✓Diamond Bank Plc

✓Fidelity Bank Plc

✓Honyflour Nigeria Plc

✓National salt company plc

✓GTassure

✓Union dicon salt plc

✓National aviation handling company plc

✓IBTC chartered bank plc

✓Academy Press Nigeria Plc

✓Trans-NationWide Express PLC

List of some Nigerian banks and websites

http://www.firstbanknigeria.com

http://www.ubagroup.com

http://www.zenithbank.com

http://www.gtbank.com

Other Useful Resources

http://www.sec.gov.ng : securities and exchange commission.

http://www.zenithbank.com/pricelist.cfm :Nigerian Daily stock updates.

http://www.nigerianstockexchange.com

http://www.cashcraft.com : Market updates and Analysis.

http://www.proshareng.com : Market updates and Analysis.

http://www.cscsnigerialtd.com : (CSCS) Limited is a subsidiary of The Nigerian Stock Exchange (NSE) as well as the Clearing House of the Nigerian Stock Market.

http://www.247BroadStreet.com:
The only Nigerian website that teaches you a

simple, step-by-step strategy that can help you profit in the Nigerian stock market.

Common Stock Market Terms

Annual Report

A report that public companies are required to file annually. It describes past years' financial results and plans for the coming year. Annual reports include information about a company's assets, liabilities, earnings, profits, and other year-end statistics.

Averaging

The process of gradually buying more and more securities in a declining market (or selling in a rising market) in order to level out the purchase (or sale) price.

Blue Chip

A company that has a history of solid earnings, regular and increasing dividends, and an impeccable balance sheet.

Breakout

When the price of a stock surpasses its initial high (resistance level) or falls below the initial low (support level), it is termed as break out in technical analysis.

Director Dealings

When directors buy or sell shares in their company.

Elliott Wave Theory

Created by Ralph Elliot in the 1930's, it assumes stock prices can be predicted by observing the various stages of waves that take place in its price cycle.

Oversubscribed

A company may offer for sale a certain number of shares. If applications are received for shares in excess of the number offered, the issue is termed as oversubscribed.

To do list for effective trading in Nigerian stock market

Obtain a Post Office or Residential Address in Nigeria.

- ✓ Engage the services of a Nigerian stock broker by opening an account with them. Ensure you obtain a personal CSCS clearing house number (CHN).
- ✓ Register as a new user through your Nigerian stock broker.
- ✓ Complete and submit a CSCS form through your Nigerian stock broker
- ✓ Fund your stock broking account
- ✓ Start buying shares aggressively but wisely
- ✓ Open a Nigerian Bank current or Verified / Referenced Savings account

- ✓ Purchase additional shares when Dividends or Bonuses are declared.
- ✓ Research and invest in companies with good management and products.
- ✓ Invest in both high-yield shares for an increased dividend and growth shares for high appreciation.
- ✓ When a stock has gone up it never hurts to take your cost off the table and ride the rest.

A Closing Thought about Investing in Nigeria

A wise investor will take what scares others away and convert it into an opportunity. Nigeria isn't always a politically stable country and is definitely a study in extremes. Lagos is a combination of extremely rich areas and extreme poverty but it still is one of the most expensive cities in the world.

A few miles out of Lagos, and you are in a completely different world, turning the clock back a hundred years. However, it is these extremes and these differences that make it an ideal country to invest in.

First of all, the Nigerian people are taking a long-term view and have understood that low labour costs make the country highly attractive to multi-national companies looking to open up manufacturing centers,
which is clear since there are already quite a few large international companies present in Nigeria.

This means the country needs improved infrastructure and to be basically brought into the 21st century.

This means there is amazing potential for an investor who can look into the future and see the unrest as an opportunity to buy into the stock market at bargain prices and subsequently watch their investment grow as Nigeria becomes Africa's central economic hub.

Have You Read?

Building Wealth with Dividend Stocks in the Nigerian Stock Market (Dividends - Stocks Secret Weapon)

This book is for the modern investor that wants to be in control of their financial future. Building Wealth with Dividend Stocks in the Nigerian stock market is a gem...packed with wise, down-to-earth advice for investors.

www.ingramcontent.com/pod-product-compliance
Lightning Source LLC
Chambersburg PA
CBHW071645170526
45166CB00003B/1439
9781469921914